Wir Spielen Zusammen

20 Games to Play with Children to Encourage and Reinforce German Language and Vocabulary

Kathy Williams
Amanda Doyle

We hope you and your pupils enjoy playing the games in this book. Brilliant Publications publishes many other books for teaching modern foreign languages. To find out more details on any of the titles listed below, please log onto our website: www.brilliantpublications.co.uk.

100+ Fun Ideas for Practising Modern Foreign Languages in the Primary Classroom	978-1-903853-98-6
More Fun Ideas for Advancing Modern Foreign Languages in the Primary Classroom	978-1-905780-72-3
Das ist Deutsch	978-1-905780-15-0
German Pen Pals Made Easy	978-1-905780-43-3
Deutsch-Lotto	978-1-905780-46-4
German Festivals and Traditions	978-1-905780-52-5
Gute Idee	978-1-905780-65-5
Singt mit Uns	978-1-905780-78-5
Chantez Plus Fort!	978-1-903853-37-5
Hexagonie 1	978-1-905780-59-4
Hexagonie 2	978-1-905780-18-1
C'est Français!	978-1-903853-02-3
J'aime Chanter!	978-1-905780-11-2
J'aime Parler!	978-1-905780-12-9
Jouons Tous Ensemble	978-1-903853-81-8
French Pen Pals Made Easy	978-1-905780-10-5
Loto Français	978-1-905780-45-7
French Festivals and Traditions	978-1-905780-44-0
Bonne Idée	978-1-905780-62-4
¡Es Español!	978-1-903853-64-1
Juguemos Todos Juntos	978-1-903853-95-5
¡Vamos a Cantar!	978-1-905780-13-6
Spanish Pen Pals Made Easy	978-1-905780-42-6
Lotto en Español	978-1-905780-47-1
Spanish Festivals and Traditions	978-1-905780-53-2
Buena Idea	978-1-905780-63-1
Giochiamo Tutti Insieme	978-1-903853-96-2
Lotto in Italiano	978-1-905780-48-8
Buon'Idea	978-1-905780-64-8

Published by Brilliant Publications
Unit 10
Sparrow Hall Farm
Edlesborough
Dunstable
Bedfordshire
LU6 2ES, UK

email: info@brilliantpublications.co.uk
website: www.brilliantpublications.co.uk

General information enquiries:
Tel: 01525 222292

The name Brilliant Publications and the logo are registered trademarks.

Written by Kathy Williams and Amanda Doyle
Cover and inside illustrations by Chantal Kees

Printed in the UK

© Kathy Williams and Amanda Doyle 2006

Printed ISBN: 978-1-903853-97-9
ebook ISBN: 978-0-85747-201-4

First published 2006. Reprinted 2009 and 2010.
10 9 8 7 6 5 4 3

The right of Kathy Williams and Amanda Doyle to be identified as the authors of this work has been asserted by them in accordance with the Copyright, Designs and Patents Act 1988.

Pages 10, 12–13, 15–17, 20, 22, 24, 26–28, 30–31, 33–34, 36–37, 39, 41–42, 44, 47–48, 50 and 52 may be photocopied by the purchasing institution or individual teachers for classroom use only, without consent from the publisher and without declaration to the Publishers Licensing Society. No other part of this book may be reproduced in any other form or for any other purpose, without the prior permission of the publisher.

Contents

All the games involve speaking, and most can be adapted to practise alternative language. See individual game descriptions for ideas.

	Language focus	Page
Introduction		4

Games involving speech and action

Guten Tag ball game	introductions	5
Colour relay	colours	6
Slap down numbers	numbers	7
Calling all animals	animals	8

Games particularly involving writing/spelling

Domino months	months	9–10
Write back	numbers	11–13
Rhyming pairs	familiar words	14–17
Spelling snake	any language	18–20
Sort yourself out	familiar words	21–22
Silly animals	animals and colours	23–24

Games involving cards/boards and speech/writing

Wacky meals	food	25–28
House designers	rooms	29–31
Super sporty week	sports/days	32–34
Weather reporters	weather	35–37
Triple time	time	38–39
The best/worst day ever at school	school subjects/time	40–42
Like it or not	likes and dislikes	43–44
A tour of Germany	transport/places in Germany	45–48
Quiz corners	any language	49–50
Rock, paper, scissors	any language	51–52

Introduction

The games in this book are designed to complement language teaching and learning, either in the classroom or at home. They are fun to play, and there is no age limit – children and adults alike can enjoy the different types of games.

Each game concentrates on one or two specific language areas. Many of the games can be adapted to practise other language vocabulary as appropriate.

All the games encourage speaking and listening. The skills of reading and writing are emphasized to different degrees in the different games.

The instructions for each game set out:
- the objectives for the game
- how to set it up
- how to play it
- extensions/variations

Some of the games require cards and boards and these are provided as photocopiable resource pages. It is a good idea to allow some time to prepare the items needed for each game before introducing them into play. If the playing cards and boards are photocopied onto thin card and laminated, you will be able to use them again and again for many years.

Guten Tag ball game

Action game

Objectives
- To practise key introduction words
- Game can be extended to include other introduction phrases as required

Schlüsselwörter – Key words
guten Tag	hello
auf Wiedersehen	goodbye
wie geht's?	how are you?
gut, danke	I'm fine, thank you
ich heiße …	my name is …

Setting up the game
- You need two or more different coloured balls.

How to play the game

1. Pupils stand in two lines facing each other. The end pupil starts with one of the balls, and throws it to the pupil opposite. That person then throws the ball to the pupil diagonally opposite, who throws it this time to the person directly opposite and so on. The ball thus makes its way in a zig-zag along the two lines.
2. While throwing and catching the ball, each pupil must say 'Guten Tag'. Using a different coloured ball, repeat the game, but this time say 'Auf Wiedersehen'.
3. Now, tell the children to take note of the colour of the ball. Using the red ball, for instance, they say 'Guten Tag', and with the blue ball they say 'Auf Wiedersehen'.
4. Start the game off with one ball again, then introduce the other ball after a couple of throws. This makes them think about which word they are saying! You could introduce further coloured balls with 'Wie geht's?', 'Gut, danke', 'Ich heiße …'. Try as many as the group can manage!
5. As a rounding-up test, stand in a large circle, and pick a pupil to hold the coloured balls in the centre. They then throw the balls (gently!) to pupils at random who must say the appropriate phrase for that colour of ball as it is thrown. Younger pupils may find that concentrating on more than two colours/phrases at once is too difficult, but older groups will enjoy the challenge of several colours/phrases in this game.

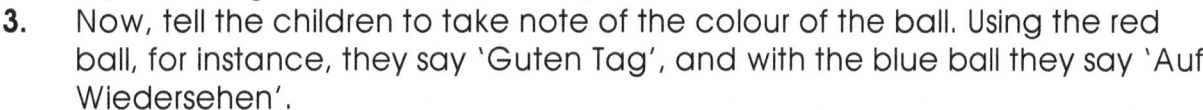

Extensions/variations
- Adapt the game to practise vocabulary groups; each time a player catches the ball the pupil must say a different animal word/colour/food item.
- Use the ball throwing idea to practise lists of words, passing the ball up and down the line or in a circle; practise the alphabet in German/days/months/numbers.

Colour relay

Action game

Objective
- To practise saying colour words and respond by picking up the correct colour from a choice

Schlüsselwörter – Key words
rot	red
weiß	white
blau	blue
schwarz	black
grün	green
rosa	pink
gelb	yellow
braun	brown
orange	orange
grau	grey

Setting up the game
- Pupils play in teams.
- You will need several items of different colours, the same number of items for each team.
- The game is best played in a large space so that the participants can run back and forth.

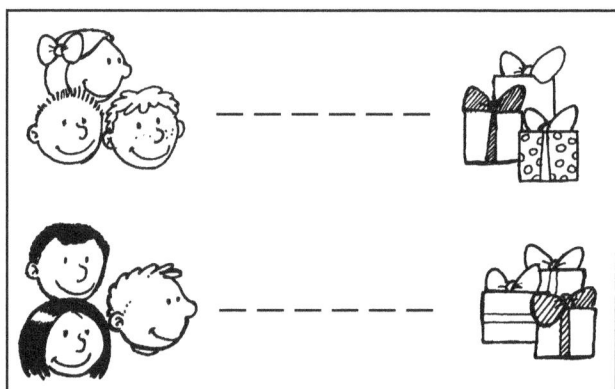

How to play the game
1. Place sets of coloured items in piles at one end of the room (or space you are playing in).
2. The teams line up opposite the coloured items so that they can race against each other in a back-and-forth relay.
3. The teacher calls out the first colour to start the race.
4. The first team member from each team runs to collect that coloured item from their team pile, and returns to the team.
5. On their return they say another colour (in German) to be picked up. The next player runs to collect that coloured item, returns to the rest of the team and says the next colour to be picked up.
6. The game continues in this way, with players joining the back of the line on their return to the team, storing all the items at the back of the line, until all the coloured items have been collected.
7. The winning team is the one that successfully collects all the items first. It is a good idea to have three or four small teams, with extra helpers to monitor the teams, so that everyone gets more than one turn, and you can listen carefully to the players saying the colours in GERMAN. You could have a rule that anyone heard saying the wrong colour, or not using German, has to run back and forth again (without picking up another item) before the next player has a turn.

Extension/variation
- To make the game more challenging pupils could say two or three colours at once, with plenty of items in the pile to choose from.

Wir Spielen Zusammen

Slap down numbers
Action game

Objectives
- To practise saying the numbers one to ten
- To listen carefully
- To respond quickly to recognition of numbers in German

Schüsselwörter – Key words
eins	one
zwei	two
drei	three
vier	four
fünf	five
sechs	six
sieben	seven
acht	eight
neun	nine
zehn	ten

Setting up the game
- Players are in pairs, sitting at a table, or where they can put their hands down quickly onto a flat surface.

How to play the game
1. Toss a coin to decide who starts. Both players have their hands on their heads to begin the game.
2. Choose one player to start first. Both players count together in German slowly.
3. When the counting reaches the number that player one has decided to stop at, he slaps his hands down, and spreads out the appropriate number of fingers on the table. For example the counting goes: 'eins ... zwei ... drei ...' but on 'vier' he slaps his hand down showing four fingers. Encourage the children to use both hands.
4. Player two must respond as quickly as possible by putting her hands down too, BUT she too must only put down the correct number of fingers, i.e. in this case only four.
5. If she puts the correct number of fingers down, then she becomes the caller. If she is not correct then player one continues to make the number choices.

Extension/variation
- The game can be made more challenging by counting up in twos, by counting backwards or by counting very quickly.

Calling all animals

Action game

Objective
- To practise saying animal words

Schlüsselwörter – Key words
Katze (f)	cat
Maus (f)	mouse
Hund (m)	dog
Spinne (f)	spider
Pferd (n)	horse
Frosch (m)	frog
Kaninchen (n)	rabbit
Fisch (m)	fish
Vogel (m)	bird
Meerschweinchen (n)	guinea-pig

Setting up the game
- Any number of pupils can play. Each player can have a different animal name given to them if there are 10 or less players; if there are more players the animal words can be used more than once.
- You need enough space for the group to form a circle.

How to play the game
1. The group forms a circle and one pupil is chosen at random to be 'it', in the middle of the circle.
2. All the animal words should be introduced and practised first so that everyone is familiar with the words.
3. Each player is then given an animal name. The whole group hears the names being given out and they can all practise each word as it is introduced. Make sure that everyone knows exactly how to say what they are, and that the person in the middle can say all the animal words (some reminding might be needed).
4. The player who is 'it' decides on an animal name to say and says it aloud three times in succession.
5. The aim of the game is for the person who has been given that animal name to join in and say their name once but before the 'it' person has finished saying it three times! If the 'animal' succeeds, he/she is then 'it' instead. If the 'it' person manages to say the word three times before the person with that animal name has said his name once, the player in the middle stays as 'it'. Everyone who manages to be 'it' must aim to stay there as long as possible, and all the others must try to get him/her out.
6. If the circle players cannot join in before their names are said three times, adjust to saying the name five times (sometimes needed for younger children).

Extensions/variations
- This game is very adaptable as it can be played with any vocabulary that you wish to practise, e.g. buildings, food, parts of the body. It works well with German girls'/boys' names.
- Another way to play is for you to spell the animal word out, either in German or English. The player who thinks that the animal name is theirs has to run around the outside of the circle back to their place before you finish spelling the word (do it slowly to give them a chance!), and say the word to make sure they were right to run.

Wir Spielen Zusammen

Domino months

Spelling game

Objective
- To practise the months in German with particular emphasis on word recognition in writing

Setting up the game
- Pupils can either play in pairs or groups with one set of dominoes (page 10) per pair.
- The dominoes could be coloured, decorated, and laminated and/or mounted on card before use.

Schlüsselwörter – Key words
Januar	January
Februar	February
März	March
April	April
Mai	May
Juni	June
Juli	July
August	August
September	September
Oktober	October
November	November
Dezember	December

How to play the game
1. Place the dominoes face down in front of the players with one domino upturned to start the game. The aim of the game is to match the dominoes to make complete month words.
2. Players each take five dominoes at random and look at them without revealing them to their opponent(s). The rest of the dominoes are put in a pile on the table.
3. One player takes a turn first, trying to complete a month word by placing one of his dominoes before or after the starting domino. Dominoes can be placed at right angles so the words do not have to go in one continuous straight line. If the first player cannot go, the other player(s) take their turn. If none of the players can place a domino, then the first player picks one up from the pile and plays the card if it completes a domino month. Play continues with players either putting down a domino or picking one up from the pile.
4. The winner is the player who uses up all of their dominoes first, or who has the least number of cards left. It isn't always possible to carry on until all the dominoes have been put down. In the case of a tie-break, maybe add the number of letters on each card together, the person with the least being the winner!
5. You will need to monitor correct positioning of the dominoes to ensure correct word completion. Saying the names of the months out loud as they are completed helps to link the written and spoken words.

Domino months

Enlarge photocopy at 115% onto thin card and cut out.

tober	Nov	ember	Ju	tember	Ju
ember	Dez	li	Ok	uar	Sep
tober	Ap	ril	Mä	ni	Feb
ruar	Ma	i	Ju	ust	Jan
uar	Feb	ni	Ok	ruar	Ju
rz	Jan	rz	Jan	ust	Mä
uar	Aug	li	Aug	li	Ju

Wir Spielen Zusammen

Write back

Spelling game

Objectives
- To reinforce knowledge of numbers up to twenty
- Version 1 practises recognition of number words. Version 2 reinforces the spellings of the numbers

Setting up the game
- Pupils play in pairs using one of the grids from number sheet (page 12) per pair, or one customized in advance to practise specific numbers or words (page 13).
- The children will need some counters or coins.

Schüsselwörter – Key words

eins	one
zwei	two
drei	three
vier	four
fünf	five
sechs	six
sieben	seven
acht	eight
neun	nine
zehn	ten
elf	eleven
zwölf	twelve
dreizehn	thirteen
vierzehn	fourteen
fünfzehn	fifteen
sechszehn	sixteen
siebzehn	seventeen
achtzehn	eighteen
neunzehn	nineteen
zwanzig	twenty

How to play the game
Version 1
1. The players have a number grid in front of them. Depending on their skill, this can be either A, B or C (from page 12) or one you have custom made using page 13.
2. Player one looks at the grid, decides on a number, but does not tell their partner. Using a finger, player one gently taps out that amount on their partner's back.
3. The partner then places a counter on the correct number on the grid and recites the number in German.
4. The game continues with each player taking turns until all the numbers are covered.

Version 2
1. The players have a grid as in version 1, but instead of tapping the required number of times for their partner to recognize, they must slowly spell out the word on their partner's back. It is best to 'draw' one letter at a time, rather than write the whole word in joined-up writing. However, the whole word technique works well with older or more able pupils.
2. As before, the player on whose back the word is written must place their counter on the correct word on the grid, saying it in German.

Extension/variation
- This game can be adapted to reinforce spellings in any language area using the blank grid to set out the language to be practised. Alternatively, the 'receiving' player writes down what they think has been spelled on their back onto a blank grid.

© Kathy Williams and Amanda Doyle

Wir Spielen Zusammen

Write back number grid

Photocopy one grid per pair (can use either Grid A, B or C)

Grid A

eins	zwei	drei	vier	fünf
sechs	sieben	acht	neun	zehn

Grid B

eins	zwei	drei	vier	fünf
sechs	sieben	acht	neun	zehn
elf	zwölf	dreizehn	vierzehn	fünfzehn
sechszehn	siebzehn	achtzehn	neunzehn	zwanzig

Grid C

elf	zwölf	dreizehn	vierzehn	fünfzehn
sechszehn	siebzehn	achtzehn	neunzehn	zwanzig

This page may be photocopied for use by the purchasing institution only.

Wir Spielen Zusammen

Write back blank number grid

Use this to prepare the language that you want to practise, or use the grid to write your answers in.

Grid A

Grid B

Grid C

Rhyming pairs

Spelling game

Objectives
- To facilitate close examination of familiar words in their written form
- To introduce the concept of using some word endings to help identify gender
- Saying the words out loud links the spelling patterns with pronunciation

Schüsselwörter – Key words
Tisch (m)	table
Fisch (m)	fish
Maus (f)	mouse
Haus (n)	house
Mund (m)	mouth
Hund (m)	dog
Mutter (f)	mother
Vater (m)	father
sonnig	sunny
windig	windy
Hose (f)	trousers
Katze (f)	cat
Limonade (f)	lemonade
Schokolade (f)	chocolate
Bein (n)	leg
Wein (m)	wine
Kartoffel (f)	potato
Apfel (m)	apple

Setting up the game
- You need to photocopy and cut out the rhyme cards (pages 15–16).
- The children will need some counters or coins.
- Players play in groups of three. Each pupil will need to pick a picture board from the selection (pages 16–17).

How to play the game
1. All the cards are placed face down and spread out on the table in front of the players.
2. The game is played as a matching pictures pairs game, only this time the matching pairs are rhyming written words.
3. Players must take turns to turn over two cards at random.
4. If they have a rhyming pair they say the two words.
5. If the pair does not rhyme they turn the cards back over and try to remember for next time where each card is.
6. When a player finds a matching pair he/she looks to see if the pair is pictured on their board.
7. If it is, they place counters or coins on the appropriate pictures and put the cards to one side. If the cards aren't pictured, he/she puts them back in the middle of the table, face down.
8. The winner is the player who completes their board first.

Extension/variation
- Players could play the game using boards and words they have created themselves. They could use vocabulary they already know (chosen either individually or as a group) or use dictionaries to look up new words.

Rhyming pairs game cards

Tisch	Fisch
Maus	Haus
Mund	Hund
Mutter	Vater
sonnig	windig
Hose	Katze

Rhyming pairs game cards

Limonade	Schokolade
Bein	Wein
Kartoffel	Apfel

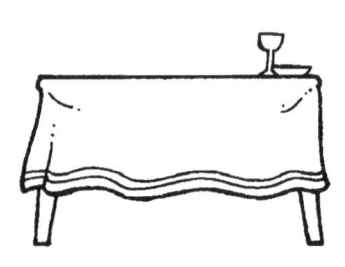 

This page may be photocopied for use by the purchasing institution only.

Wir Spielen Zusammen

Rhyming pairs board

Wir Spielen Zusammen

Spelling snake

Spelling game

Objective
- To encourage the use of a specific area of vocabulary or to give players the opportunity to use any language that they know

Setting up the game
- This game can be played with four or more people.
- Each child needs a blank copy of the 'spelling snake' (page 20).

How to play the game
1. Start as a whole group and brainstorm a large number of words within a vocabulary area, or several areas. At the end of this session, write these words, correctly spelled onto the board, or provide a prepared list that contains the words you elicited from the players. (This list would benefit from containing words that start or finish with a variety of letters – take care that not all your words end in the letter 'e' for example).
2. Give the players a couple of minutes to study the words, then remove them from view.
3. Each player writes one word of their choice from the target list into the first section of their spelling snake (see 'Hier anfangen').
4. All players then simultaneously pass the snake on to another player, and here you must ensure random exchanges.
5. Using the final letter of the first word, each player must then write in a new word from the list, and then pass the snake on as before.
6. If a player cannot write a word starting with the last letter (which is often not possible), he/she writes a new word that is unconnected and passes on the snake as before.
7. The class continue to write on and pass around the snakes until all the spaces are full. You can make the game easier by allowing repeats of the same word, or harder by having a 'no repeats' rule.
8. When the snakes are complete, and there may be some which take longer than others, the snake that each player ends with becomes the one which will score or lose them points.

To score points

- Ask each player to check the words on his snake against the original list. A correctly spelled word gets 2 points. Add on an extra 1 point for every word that starts with the last letter of the previous one. The winner is the player with the highest total of points at the end.
- If you tell the players how the scoring works before they start to play it will encourage everyone to spell correctly as they do not know which snake they will have at the end.

Extensions/variations

- Alternatively, tell the players that they are going to be able to use any words they like during the game, but that spelling must be correct. In this case play the game and then include a follow-up session to go over the words and their spellings together.
- If players do not have time to study the words immediately before the game, this game can be used to test spelling knowledge of a preset group of words.

Spelling snake

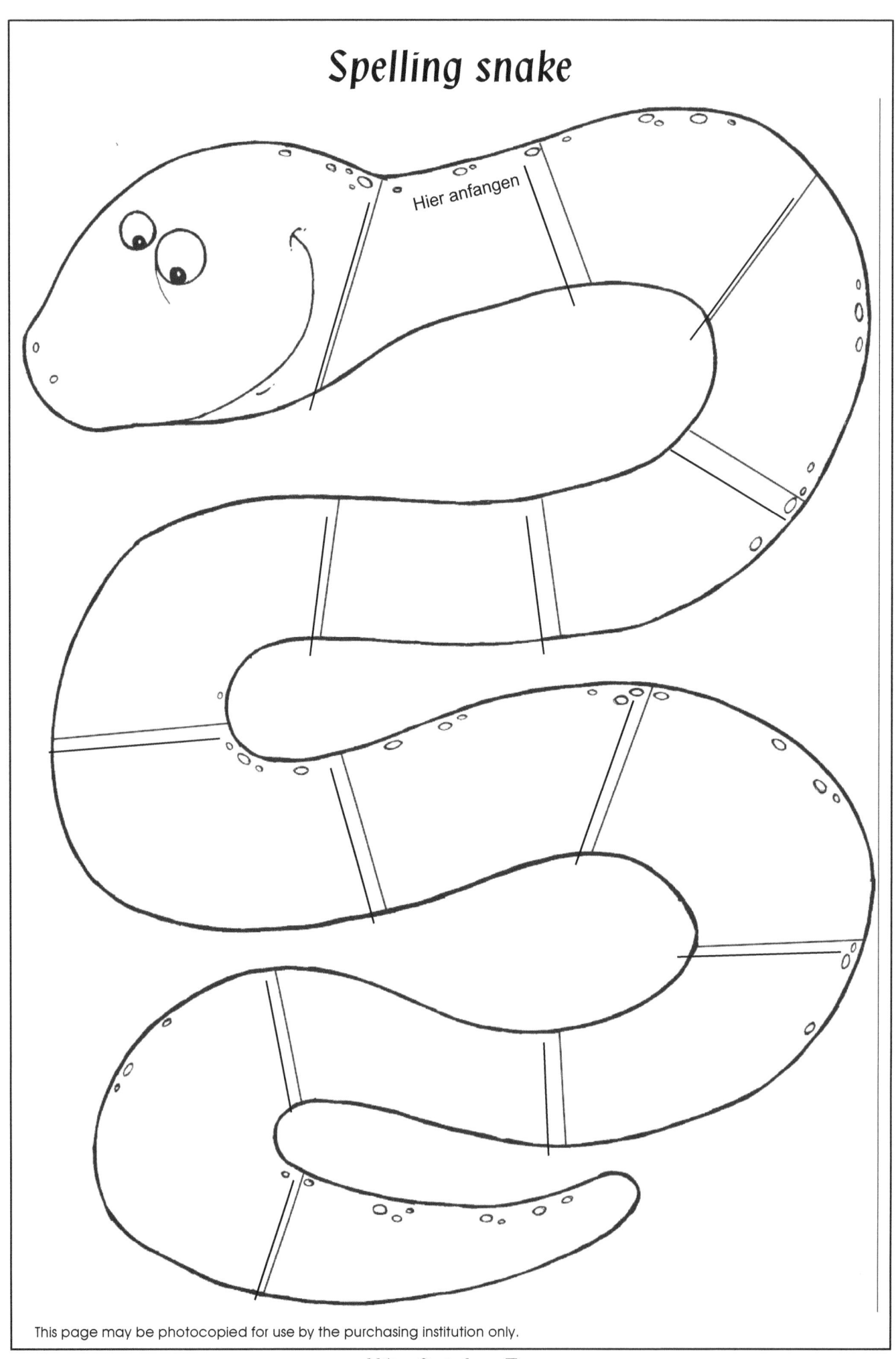

Hier anfangen

This page may be photocopied for use by the purchasing institution only.

Wir Spielen Zusammen

Sort yourself out

Spelling game

Objective
- To arrange sets of words beginning with the same letter into alphabetical order

Setting up the game
- You need 'sort yourself out' list of words (page 22) and blank sheets for the children's answers.
- Children will need some scissors and some pens/pencils.
- Children play in pairs.

How to play the game
1. Cut the word lists into separate columns and give each pair of children one list.
2. The children cut the words out individually into strips and mix them up.
3. They then must try to put their words into alphabetical order. They write down the words and their meanings, guessing for those they don't know. You could set a time limit for this task.
4. At the end of the allotted time, the teacher reads out or writes down the correct alphabetical order for each list and the word meanings. Players get a point for every correct position in the list and a point for each correct meaning.

Extension/variation
- The game can be played again using a different set of words or you could create your own list. This game is very useful for checking the pupils' understanding of vocabulary practised.

Schlüsselwörter – Key words

Bad (n)	bath
Banane (f)	banana
Bär (m)	bear
Bein (n)	leg
blau	blue
braun	brown
Dame (f)	lady
danke	thank you
Dezember	December
Dienstag	Tuesday
Donnerstag	Thursday
drei	three
Haare (n, pl)	hair
Hamster (m)	hamster
Hand (f)	hand
Haus (n)	house
Hose (f)	trousers
Hund (m)	dog
Mai	May
März	March
Maus (f)	mouse
Meerschweinchen (n)	guinea pig
Milch (f)	milk
Mutter (f)	mother
Name (m)	name
Nase (f)	nose
nein	no
neun	nine
Nilpferd (n)	hippopotamus
November	November
Radiergummi (m)	rubber
Rentier (n)	reindeer
rosa	pink
rot	red
Rucksack (m)	rucksack
ruhig	quiet
Schokolade (f)	chocolate
schwarz	black
Schwester (f)	sister
September	September
sonnig	sunny
Spinne (f)	spider
Tag (m)	day
tanzen	to dance
Tasse (f)	cup
Technik (f)	technology
Tisch (m)	table
Tomate (f)	tomato
Vater (m)	father
vergessen	to forget
viel	a lot
vier	four
violett	purple
Vogel (m)	bird

Sort yourself out

Bad	Dame	Haare
Banane	danke	Hamster
Bär	Dezember	Hand
Bein	Dienstag	Haus
blau	Donnerstag	Hose
braun	drei	Hund
Mai	Name	Radiergummi
März	Nase	Rentier
Maus	nein	rosa
Meerschweinchen	neun	rot
Milch	Nilpferd	Rucksack
Mutter	November	ruhig
Schokolade	Tag	Vater
schwarz	tanzen	vergessen
Schwester	Tasse	viel
September	Technik	vier
sonnig	Tisch	violett
Spinne	Tomate	Vogel

Silly animals

Spelling game

Objective
- To encourage recognition of simple sentence building rules and parts of speech, using 'ist' (is)
- To practise using animal names and colours

Setting up the game
- Prepare the game by photocopying and cutting out the word sections (page 24), one for every player or pair of players.

How to play the game
1. Give each player (or pair) a set of mixed-up word sections.
2. Discuss the parts of a sentence: noun (das Substantiv), verb (das Verb), adjective (das Adjektiv). Remind children that in German nouns always have a capital letter.
3. Demonstrate a sentence, for example 'Der Hund ist braun und weiß.'
4. Ask the players to form as many sentences as they can, by changing around the words. Look at and discuss the parts of speech and word order.
5. Ask the pupils to see what 'silly' sentences they can create. Remember that the 'silly' sentences should still be formed correctly, e.g. 'Das Pferd ist blau und orange.'

Schlüsselwörter – Key words

die Katze	the cat
die Maus	the mouse
der Hund	the dog
die Spinne	the spider
das Pferd	the horse
der Frosch	the frog
das Kaninchen	the rabbit
der Fisch	the fish
der Vogel	the bird
das Meerschweinchen	the guinea pig
ist	is
und	and
rot	red
weiß	white
blau	blue
schwarz	black
grün	green
rosa	pink
gelb	yellow
braun	brown
orange	orange
grau	grey

Extensions/variations
- Players could draw pictures of their favourite sentences. They can then read them out to a friend, who then has to draw and colour the appropriate animal.
- Use other animals/food/rooms.

© Kathy Williams and Amanda Doyle

Wir Spielen Zusammen

Silly animals

Die Katze	ist	rot
Die Maus	und	weiß
Der Hund		blau
Die Spinne		schwarz
Das Pferd		grün
Der Frosch		rosa
Das Kaninchen		gelb
Der Fisch		braun
Der Vogel		orange
Das Meerschweinchen		grau

Wacky meals

Card game

Objective
- To recognize and use some food words, as well as the correct words for the different meal times

Setting up the game
- Players are in pairs or small groups.
- Each group will need a set of food word cards (page 27) and 'die Speisekarte' (page 28).

How to play the game
1. Each group has a set of food cards face down in front of them.
2. One player picks up a card at random and places it face up in the first 'zum Frühstück' position on the menu, saying aloud what the food item is in German.
3. The second player then picks up another card and places it on the next breakfast position, saying the food item in German. Some strange breakfast choices may be beginning to appear!
4. Players continue until all the meals are set.
5. When finished they discuss together what meals have been created using the sentence structures: 'Zum Frühstück möchte ich …' And so on.
6. Each pair or group then presents the 'wacky meals' that they have on their menus to the rest of the class.

Schlüsselwörter – Key words

zum …	for …
Frühstück (n)	breakfast
Mittagessen (n)	lunch
Abendessen (n)	dinner
möchte ich …	I would like …
Brot (n)	bread
Butter (f)	butter
Käse (m)	cheese
Schinken (m)	ham
ein Sandwich (n)	a sandwich
ein Spiegelei (n)	a fried egg
Karotten (f, pl)	carrots
Erbsen (f, pl)	peas
Kartoffeln (f, pl)	potatoes
ein Schnitzel (n)	a cutlett
ein Würstchen (n)	a sausage
Nudeln (f, pl)	pasta
Pommes Frites (pl)	chips
Schokolade (f)	chocolate
Kirschen (f, pl)	cherries
eine Banane (f)	a banana
Cola (f)	coke
Mineralwasser (n)	mineral water

Extensions/variations
- The picture cards (page 26) can be used instead of the food word cards to prompt usage of food words.
- The game can be played as a whole class if the menu sheet is enlarged. Individuals take turns to choose cards and place them or write the food item onto the menu.
- Using the same concept, make cards showing different items of clothing, and instead of a menu sheet, use places/events to dress for, for example 'In **den Ferien** trage ich … (In **the holidays** I wear …); In **der Schule** trage ich … (In **school** I wear …); Auf **einer Party** trage ich … (To **a party** I wear …).' See what funny outfits emerge! For practising food we have not used any singular masculine nouns to avoid the need to change the form due to case. If you use them for this activity you will need to change 'ein' to 'einen' in sentences such as 'Für die Ferien trage ich einen Hut.' ('For the holidays I wear a hat.')

© Kathy Williams and Amanda Doyle

Wir Spielen Zusammen

www.brilliantpublications.co.uk

Wacky meals picture cards

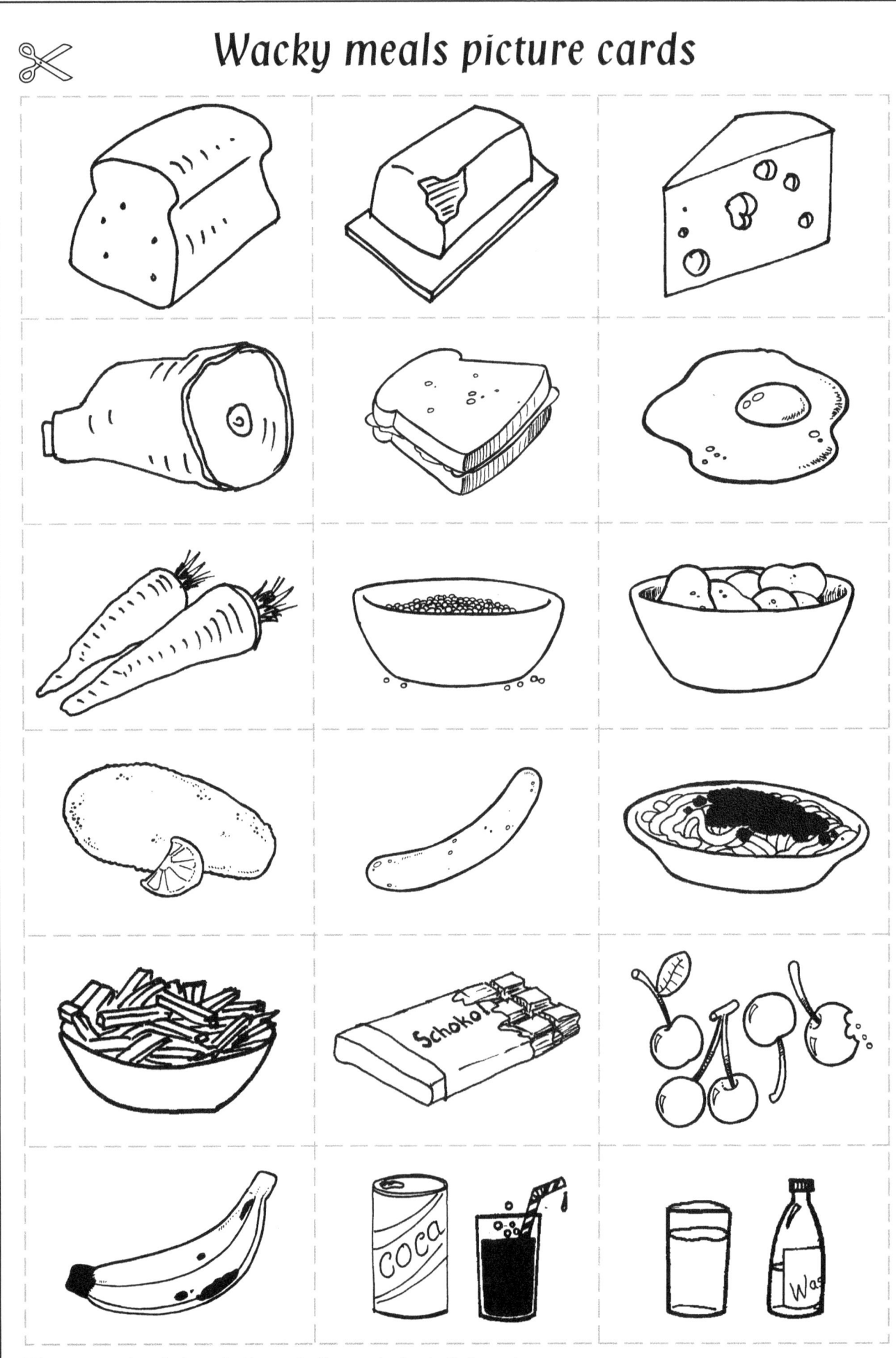

Wir Spielen Zusammen

Wacky meals food word cards

Brot	Butter	Käse
Schinken	ein Sandwich	ein Spiegelei
Karrotten	Erbsen	Kartoffeln
ein Schnitzel	ein Würstchen	Nudeln
Pommes Frites	Schokolade	Kirschen
eine Banane	Cola	Mineralwasser

Wacky meals menu sheet

Menu choices

1 Zum Frühstück	2	3
1 Zum Mittagessen	2	3
1 Zum Abendessen	2	3

This page may be photocopied for use by the purchasing institution only.

Wir Spielen Zusammen

House designers

Board/card game

Objectives
- To use the names for rooms in the house
- To communicate information about the layout of a house
- The use of 'hier' (here), 'dort' (there) and 'das ist' (that is) can also be reinforced

Schlüsselwörter – Key words
hier	here
dort	there
das ist	that is
ist	is
die Küche	the kitchen
das Wohnzimmer	the lounge
das Schlafzimmer	the bedroom
die Diele	the hall
das Badezimmer	the bathroom
die Garage	the garage
das Esszimmer	the dining room
der Dachboden	the attic

Setting up the game
- Pupils play in teams of three, with the teams racing each other.
- Two 'house design sheets' (page 30) are needed per group. Room pictures (page 31) can be used for guidance.
- A spacious room/area (two rooms could be used) to separate two of the three players in each team, so that they cannot see the other player's sheet.

How to play the game
1. One pair of players (players two and three) has a 'house design sheet', a set of room pictures, and a pen/pencil, and sits some distance away from their other team-mate, or in another room.
2. Player one in the team has a 'house design sheet' and a pen/pencil.
3. Player one starts the game by deciding which room to designate first. For example, if he/she decides that the upstairs room on the right is the bedroom, he/she writes 'das Schlafzimmer' or draws a picture of a bed inside that room.
4. When all the player ones from each competing team have made their decision the teacher tells the player twos to start.
5. Player two from each team visits his/her team-mate to find out which room has been chosen, while player three remains behind with a blank 'house design sheet'. On his return, player two tells player three what and where the room is on their design sheet, **in German, not in English!** For example, in this case, they will need to point to the upstairs right room 'hier' and say 'Das ist das Schlafzimmer.' Player three must then write in the words 'das Schlafzimmer', or draw an appropriate picture, in the correct room.
6. In the meantime player one chooses another room. Player two returns to player one to find out the whereabouts of the next room and returns to player three to relay that piece of information.
7. The winning team is the one who is first in relaying all the information correctly. Remind players that all of the information should be spoken in German, and although a picture may be drawn instead, this will only take up extra time.

Wir Spielen Zusammen

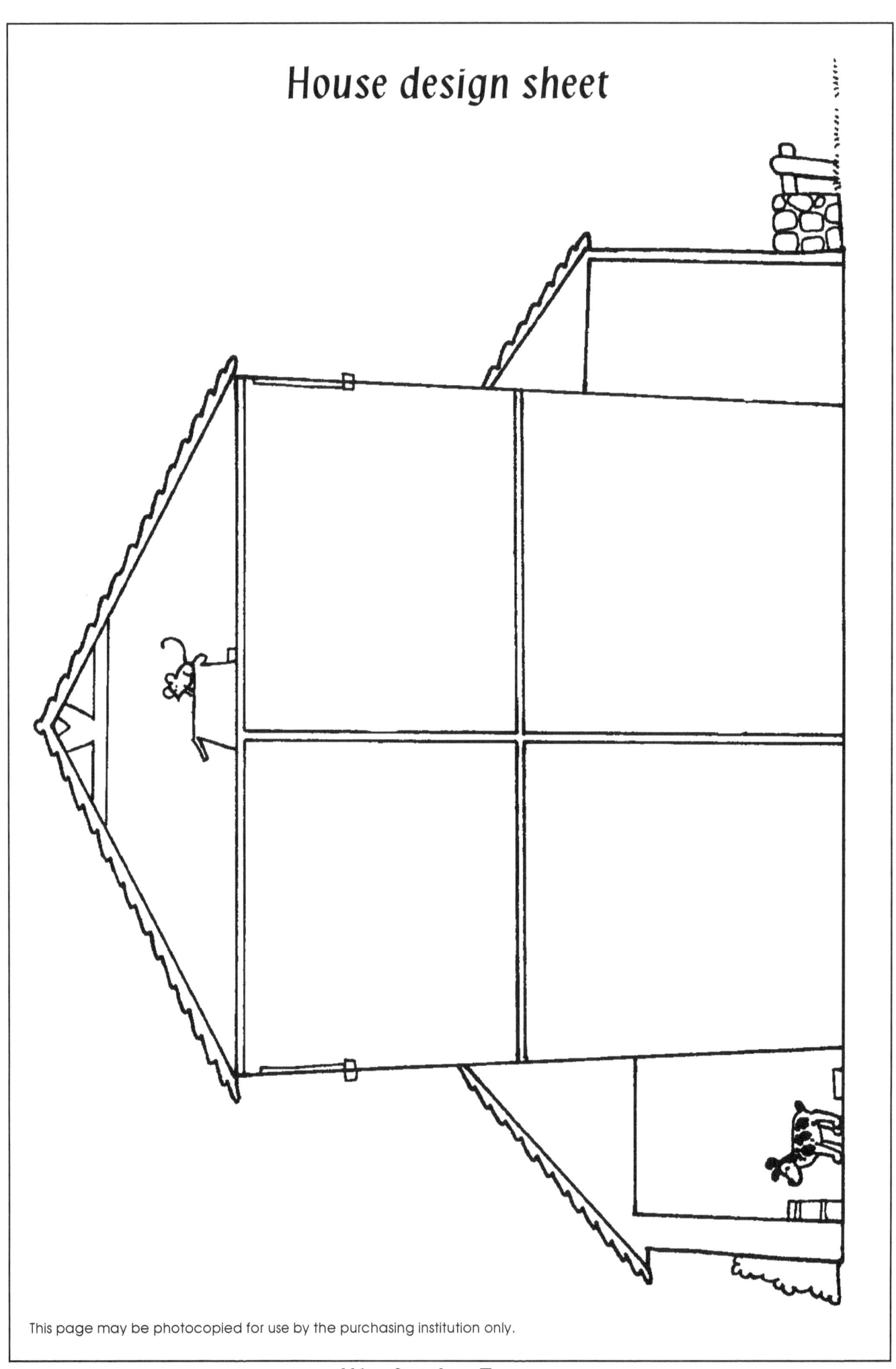

House designers room pictures

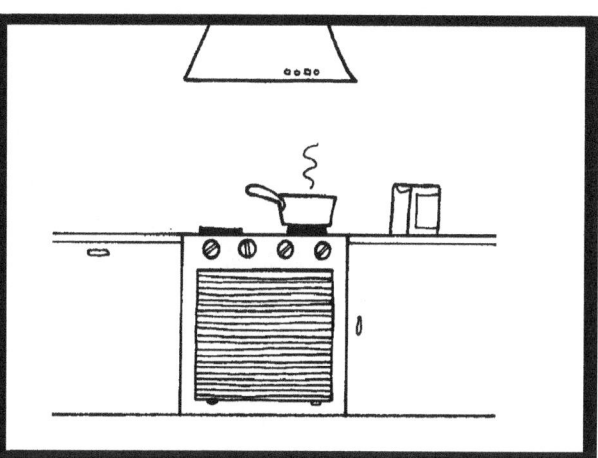

Super sporty week

Board game

Objectives
- To prompt pupils to use the phrases 'ich spiele ...', 'ich mache ...' and 'ich gehe ...' in conjunction with seven sport activities
- To practise the days of the week (extension activity)

Setting up the game
- Play in pairs or small groups with one game board (page 33) per group.
- Dice and counters are required.
- Each pupil will need a week planner (page 34).

How to play the game
1. Starting at 'Hier anfangen' one pupil throws the die and moves the counter the relevant number of places around the board. They must **say** the phrase indicated by the activity picture on the place where they land. They then write the activity onto a day of their choice on the week planner. The next pupil then takes a turn and so on.
2. Pupils continue to throw the die in turn and move repeatedly around the board, until they have landed on all the activities and chosen which day to write them in. When they land on activities already used they must still say the appropriate sentence.

Extensions/variations
- You could make the game competitive by having a time limit, or by having the first player to complete their week as the winner. If you wish all pupils to complete the week plan, encourage those who have finished quickly to listen to and help the others, until all have finished.
- As a follow-up activity pupils could present their weekly activity plans to each other or the class. You will need to tell the children that the verb goes before 'ich' when there is something else before it, for example: 'Dienstags spiele ich Fußball. Freitags gehe ich radfahren.' etc.

Schlüsselwörter – Key words

ich spiele ...	I play ...
Fußball (m)	football
Rugby (n)	rugby
Basketball (m)	basketball
Tennis (n)	tennis
ich mache ...	I do ...
Leichtathletik (f)	athletics
ich gehe ...	I go ...
radfahren	to cycle/cycling
schwimmen	to swim/swimming
Montag	Monday
Dienstag	Tuesday
Mittwoch	Wednesday
Donnerstag	Thursday
Freitag	Friday
Samstag	Saturday
Sonntag	Sunday

Wir Spielen Zusammen

Super sporty week board game

This page may be photocopied for use by the purchasing institution only.

© Kathy Williams and Amanda Doyle

Wir Spielen Zusammen

www.brilliantpublications.co.uk

Super sporty week board game

Montag	
Dienstag	
Mittwoch	
Donnerstag	
Freitag	
Samstag	
Sonntag	

This page may be photocopied for use by the purchasing institution only.

Wir Spielen Zusammen

Weather reporters

Board/card game

Objectives
- To ask and answer questions about the weather
- To reinforce the names of some principal towns in Germany

Setting up the game
- Pupils play together in pairs with one weather grid (page 36) each and a set of town and weather cards (page 37) per pair.

Schlüsselwörter – Key words

es ist sonnig	it is sunny
es ist windig	it is windy
es ist schlecht	it is bad
es ist schön	it is fine
es ist heiß	it is hot
es ist kalt	it is cold
es regnet	it is raining
es schneit	it is snowing
wie ist das Wetter?	what's the weather like?
in	at/in

How to play the game
1. Put the town cards and the weather cards in two piles, face down.
2. Using the weather grids, both players first make a weather prediction for each of their towns and tell them to their partner in German. They record their forecasts in writing or by drawing a picture in the 'weather forecast' column on the grid.
3. One player then picks up a town name card and asks what the weather is like there using 'Wie ist das Wetter in …?' e.g. 'Wie ist das Wetter in Berlin?' The town card used is put to one side.
4. The other player picks a weather card and answers using the weather pictured, e.g. 'Es regnet in Berlin.' The cards can be interpreted in a number of possible ways, for example the sun card could be 'Es ist schön / Es ist sonnig / Es ist heiß.' If this is what either player predicted they put a tick in the second column; if they were wrong they put a cross. The weather card used is returned to the bottom of the pile.
5. The players swap roles and continue asking and answering until all the towns' weather conditions have been filled in on the grid.
6. The winner is the player who scored the most ticks at the end of the game.

© Kathy Williams and Amanda Doyle

Wir Spielen Zusammen

Weather reporters town grid

Town	Weather forecast	✓ or ✗
Berlin		
Köln		
Frankfurt		
München		
Leipzig		
Bonn		
Hamburg		
Hannover		

This page may be photocopied for use by the purchasing institution only.

Wir Spielen Zusammen

Weather reports

Köln	München	Bonn	Hannover
Berlin	Frankfurt	Leipzig	Hamburg

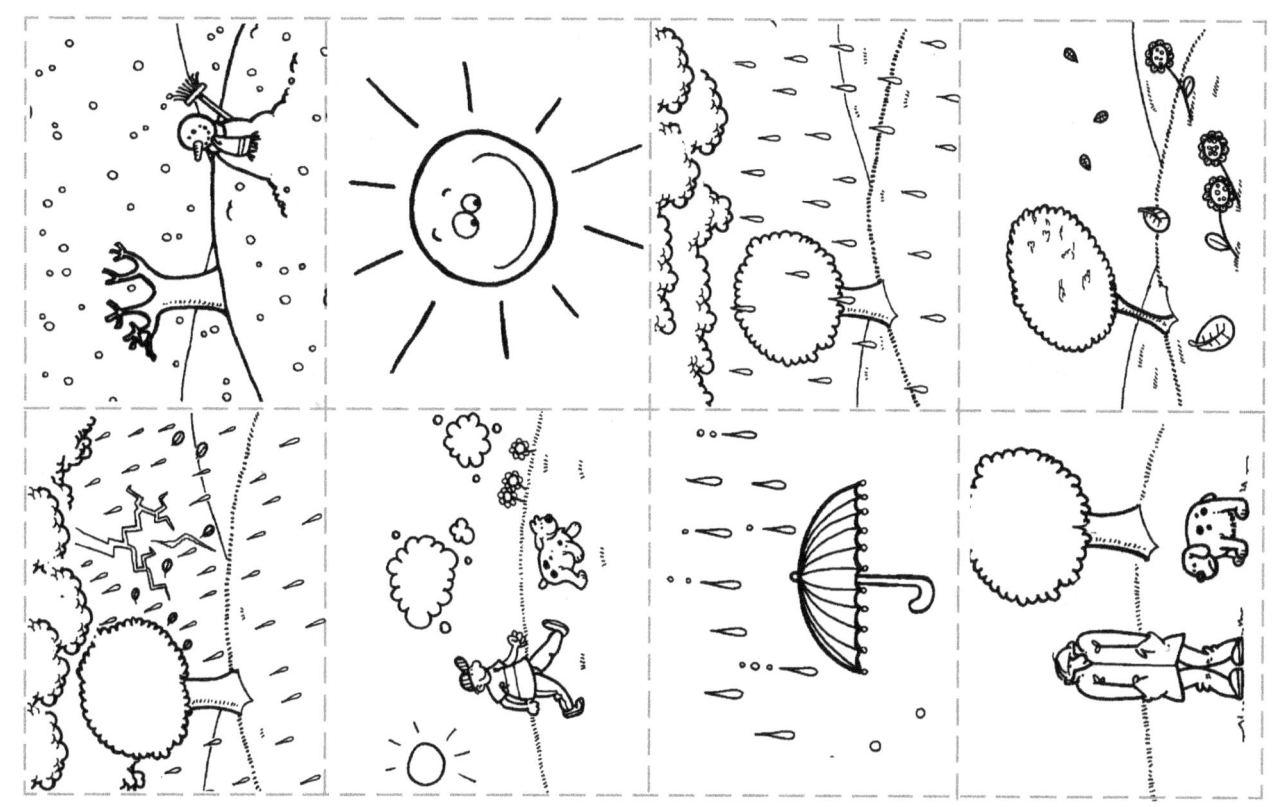

Triple time

Card game

Objectives
- To practise telling the time in German
- To reinforce understanding of digital and analogue times and the times written out in German

Schlüsselwörter – Key words
es ist …	it is …
ein Uhr	one o'clock
zwei Uhr	two o'clock
drei Uhr	three o'clock
vier Uhr	four o'clock
fünf Uhr	five o'clock
sechs Uhr	six o'clock
sieben Uhr	seven o'clock
acht Uhr	eight o'clock
neun Uhr	nine o'clock
zehn Uhr	ten o'clock
elf Uhr	eleven o'clock
Mittag	midday
Mitternacht	midnight

Setting up the game
- Pupils work in pairs.
- Pupils need one set of time cards from page 39 per pair. You could make more cards to practise other times.

How to play the game
1. In pairs, players have a set of time cards in front of them, face down on the table.
2. One player turns over three different cards, trying to find a matching set of three. If he finds three which all say the same time – in digital, analogue and in German – he keeps the set. If the three cards do not match, they are turned face down again and the other player has a turn. (The game works just like a 'pairs' game, except that the players are finding three cards.)
3. To aid the players' chances of finding a match, if they turn over two which match in one go, they keep these to one side until their next turn, when they have three chances to find the third card. If the third card is not found during that turn, they keep the pair to the side until the third is found on a further turn. If their opponent turns over the card that they are missing from their set, this card must be returned to the table, face down.
4. When the players are turning over the cards, encourage them to say the times out loud in German every time, using a whole sentence, e.g. 'Es ist fünf Uhr.'

Extension/variation
- The times are only on the hour, so that players can concentrate on their German. You could make more cards which show half past, quarter to, etc. if you feel that your pupils can manage.

It is half past ten.   Es ist halb elf.
(in German this is expressed as halfway TO the hour)

It is quarter past three.   Es ist Viertel nach drei.
It is quarter to one.   Es ist Viertel vor eins.

Triple time cards

Set 1

Es ist drei Uhr.	3:00	
Es ist neun Uhr.	9:00	
Es ist elf Uhr.	11:00	
Es ist Mittag / Mitternacht.	12:00	

Set 2

Es ist acht Uhr.	8:00	
Es ist vier Uhr.	4:00	
Es ist zwei Uhr.	2:00	
Es ist sechs Uhr.	6:00	

This page may be photocopied for use by the purchasing institution only.

© Kathy Williams and Amanda Doyle

Wir Spielen Zusammen

www.brilliantpublications.co.uk

The best/worst day ever at school
Grid game

Objectives
- To practise saying school subjects
- To practise counting
- To practise saying times on the hour

Schlüsselwörter – Key words

Deutsch (n)	German
Kunst (f)	art
Englisch (n)	English
Geschichte (f)	history
Musik (f)	music
Informatik (f)	ICT
Mathe (f)	maths
Naturwissenschaft (f)	science
eins	one
um ein Uhr	at one o'clock
um zwei Uhr	at two o'clock
drei	three
vier	four
fünf	five
sechs	six
sieben	seven
acht	eight
neun	nine
zehn	ten
elf	eleven
am Mittag	at midday
Nachmittag	afternoon

Setting up the game
- Pupils need a 'school day timetable' (page 41) each and one 'Chinese counter' per pair (page 42). Cut out the grid and fold to make the counter.
- Pupils work in pairs.

How to play the game
1. Players fill in their 'ideal' timetable first in the right-hand column of the school day timetable sheet. They then fold back this column so that they cannot see the subjects they have written.
2. Player one picks a time for a lesson from his/her timetable at random, e.g. 'drei Uhr'.
3. Player two (who has the 'Chinese counter') counts and moves the counter in and out **three** times, counting 'eins, zwei, drei'.
4. Player one then picks one of the numbers visible on the counter, in German, e.g. if five is visible he/she may pick that and say 'fünf'.
5. Player two counts and moves the counter again, this time **five** times.
6. Player one then chooses one of the visible numbers on the counter and this time player two lifts up the corresponding flap.
7. Under the flap is a school subject. Player one reads this out to player two, who then writes this into his/her timetable, in the hour that he/she originally chose (in this case 'drei Uhr'). Players must say out loud the timetable and subject as they fill this part in, e.g. 'Um drei Uhr habe ich Deutsch.'
8. The players keep swapping over roles of choosing and counting so that both players can complete their timetables.
9. When all timetables are complete the class reveal and discuss their results. The best or worst school day!

Extension/variation
- The 'Chinese counter' is a very adaptable resource that can be used for counting practice as well as having different vocabulary written inside. For example, instead of school subjects, write in buildings. The day's timetable can be filled in to say the time that each building is visited on a tour of the town. Use 'ich besichtige …' instead of 'ich habe …' (e.g. 'Um drei Uhr besichtige ich das Museum.')

Wir Spielen Zusammen

School day timetable

	habe ich ...	habe ich ...
Um 9 Uhr		
Um 10 Uhr		
Um 11 Uhr		
Um 1 Uhr		
Um 2 Uhr		
Um 3 Uhr		
Um 4 Uhr		

Chinese counter template

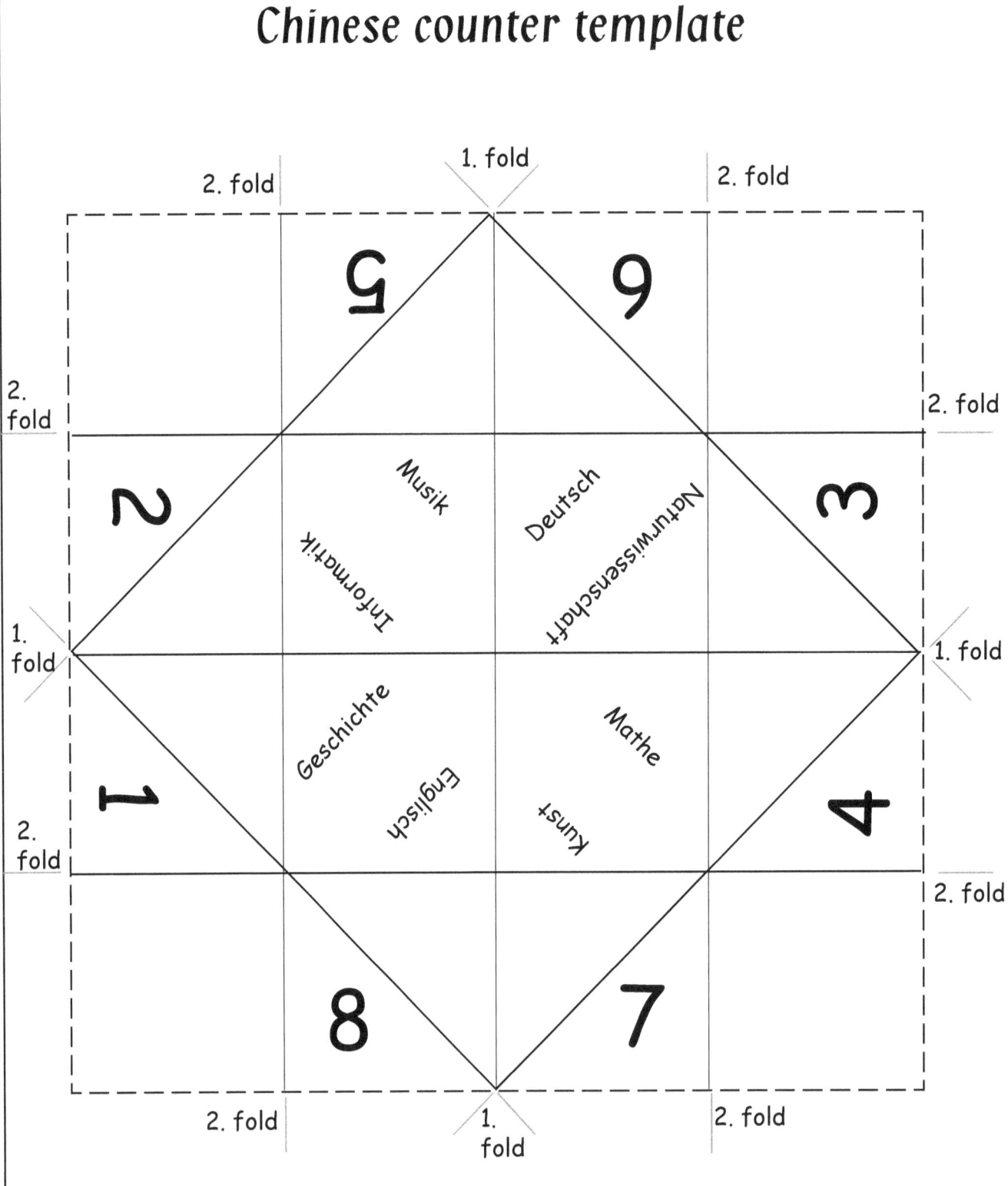

1. Fold corners **back** behind face of paper.
2. Fold corners **inward** to centre.
3. Put your thumb and forefinger of both hands into the back of the resulting square and pinch up into a point.

This page may be photocopied for use by the purchasing institution only.

Wir Spielen Zusammen

Like it or not
Board game

Objectives
- To practise saying 'ich mag ...' and 'ich mag ... nicht', while talking about school subjects

Setting up the game
- Pupils play in pairs using an enlarged photocopy of the grid (page 44), a coin, and a different coloured counter each.

How to play the game
1. The players put their counters on 'Hier anfangen'.
2. They decide who goes first by tossing a coin.
3. Player one tosses the coin – if **heads**, player one moves his/her counter to 'Ich mag ...' completing the phrase with a school subject, for example, 'Ich mag Musik.' If **tails**, player one moves to the 'Ich mag ... nicht' position instead, and completes the phrase with another subject, for example, 'Ich mag Informatik nicht.'
4. Player two then tosses the coin and moves/speaks in the same way. Both players can be on the same place on the grid at the same time.
5. They continue to move across the grid until the first player reaches the last column on the right-hand side of the board. Player two must then throw the opposite to player one's last throw, and complete the opposite phrase to avoid losing the game. For example, if player one completed the course by throwing heads and said 'Ich mag ...' then player two has to throw tails to finish, or he has automatically lost the game. If he throws tails then the game is a draw.
6. On completing the game, the players start again (and again) at 'Hier anfangen', with alternating players starting the game. They should keep a tally of how many games they win. They could play 'best of five' for example.
7. By repeating the game (at a quick pace for older pupils) the language is being continually reinforced. You could make it more challenging by saying that players must not repeat a school subject if their partner has already said it within that game. There are ten school subjects listed in the key words list, so this should be possible.

Extension/variation
- The game can be adapted to practise likes and dislikes of other things, e.g. different foods or sports. Note: in some cases you will need to use the plural form, e.g. 'ich mag Karotten' (carrots), 'ich mag **Ä**pfel nicht' (apples).

Schüsselwörter – Key words

ich mag ...	I like ...
ich mag ... nicht	I don't like ...
Deutsch (n)	German
Kunst (f)	art
Sport (m)	PE
Englisch (n)	English
Geschichte (f)	history
Erdkunde (f)	geography
Musik (f)	music
Informatik (f)	ICT
Mathe (f)	maths
Naturwissenschaft (f)	science

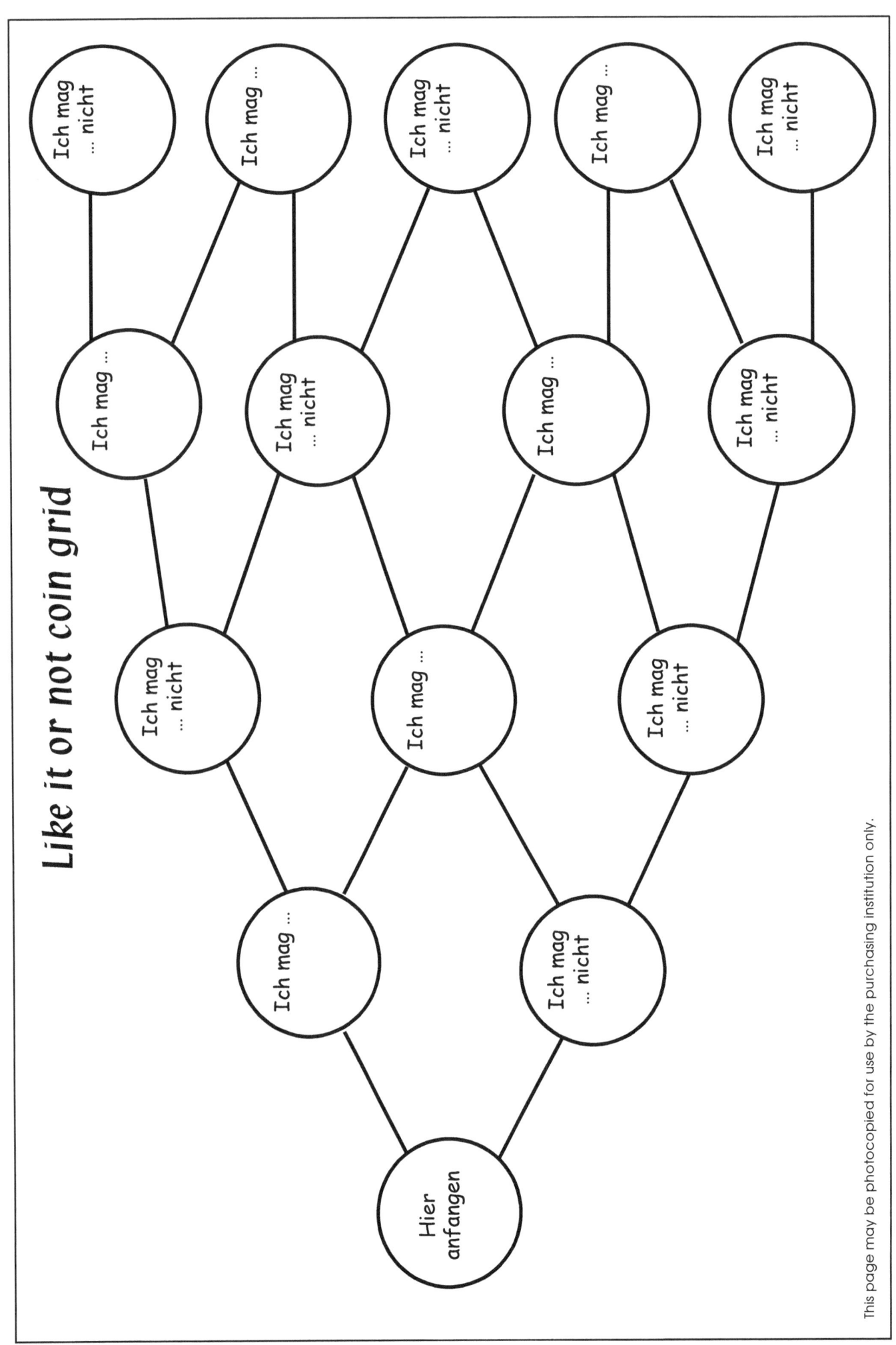

A tour of Germany

Board game

Objectives
- To practise using transport words
- To practise German word order using 'Ich fahre' + manner + 'nach' + town (ie. manner comes before place)

> **Schlüsselwörter – Key words**
> ich fahre nach ...   I am going to ...
>   Berlin, Frankfurt, Hamburg, etc.
> mit dem Bus (m)   by bus
> mit dem Schiff (n)   by boat
> mit dem Fahrrad (n)   by bike
> mit dem Auto (n)   by car
> mit dem Flugzeug (n)   by plane
> mit dem Zug (m)   by train

Setting up the game
- All players require a map (page 47) each and one die between them, made from the template (page 48). This can be coloured and assembled in advance of the game by the players.
- The same game can be played either in pairs or groups of three or four.

How to play the game
1. Make sure all the players can identify the names of the main towns featured on the map before the game begins.
2. Each player must make a round trip of Germany, from Berlin back to Berlin, via the route shown on the map.
3. The players must keep their maps hidden from the view of the other player(s). This is because in the final part of the game, points are lost if two players have chosen the same form of transport for the same leg of the tour.
4. One player starts by rolling the die. He must say aloud the form of transport that he throws, and then quietly decide which part of the route he will make using that form of transport. It can be any leg of the journey that is chosen. For example, if he threw a train picture, he could decide to travel by train between Frankfurt and Köln (Cologne). He makes a note of his choice in the itinerary table below the map, and writes down the points he has scored using the die. Take care to fill in the correct line on the points tally.
5. The next player then throws the die, and makes a choice on his travel itinerary in the same way. The game continues until each player has made a complete route around Germany. They might have thrown the same picture most of the time and made almost the whole route by car, for example. Or they may have a wide variety of modes of transport in their travel itinerary. If, however, the boat is thrown, it can only be used between Hamburg and Kiel (via the Kiel canal). If they throw a boat and this leg of the journey has already been filled in, they have to miss a turn.

To score points
- Player one starts by saying in German one of the sections of his journey, for example, 'Ich fahre mit dem Auto nach München' (Munich). The other player(s) look(s) at their maps, and if they have used the car for this section as well, then they all lose their points for this section. If only the first player has used the car here then he keeps his 1 point (on the die the car is worth 1 point).

- The next player then says one of her sections, 'Ich fahre mit dem Zug nach Leipzig.' The other players check their maps and either cross off their train and points, or leave other transport choices in place. As before, the player speaking only keeps her points if she is the only player to use the train in this part of the tour.
- When the whole route has been discussed, the winner is the player with the most points.

A tour of Germany

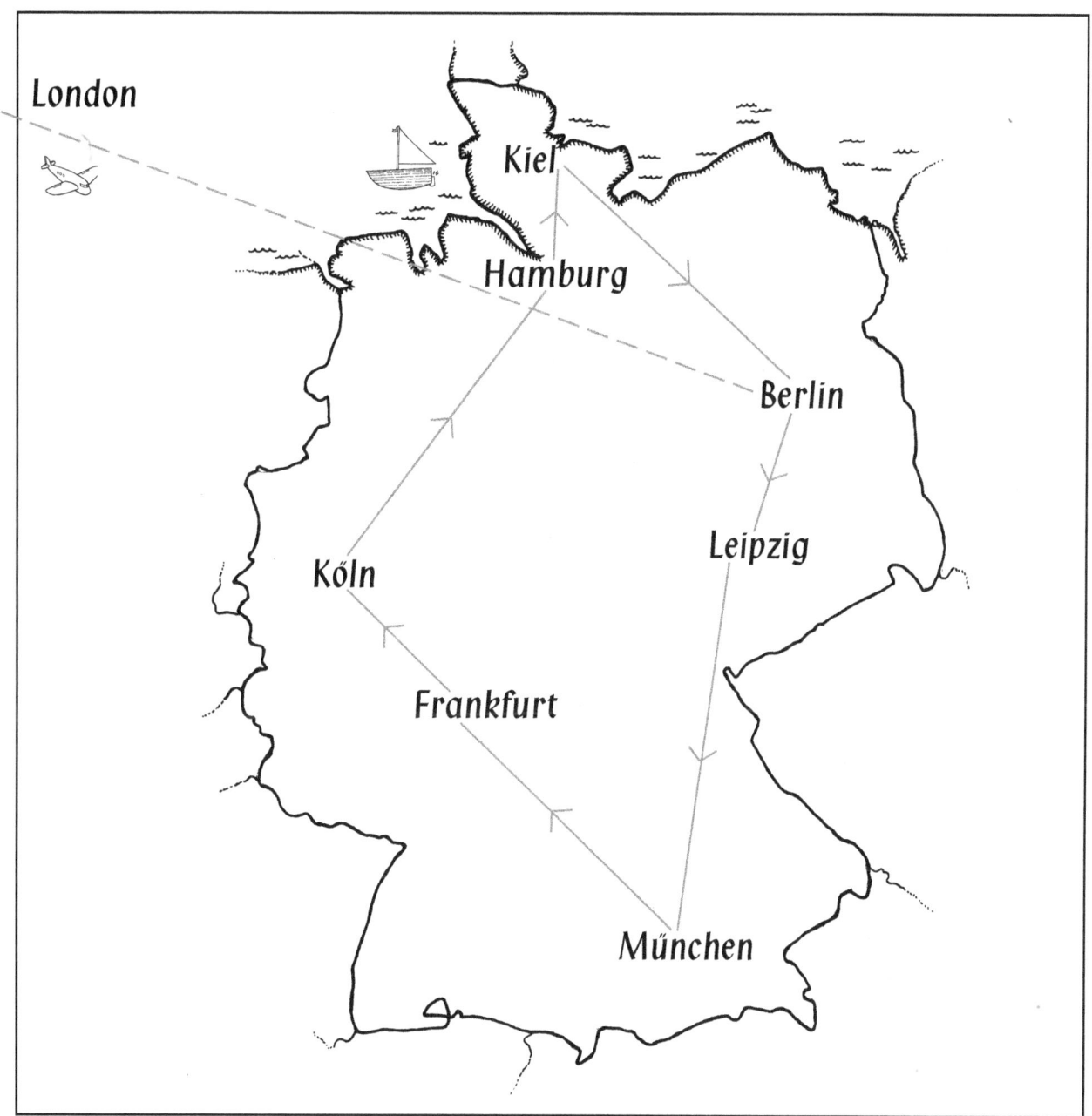

Ich fahre mit dem ....Flugzeug........ nach Berlin	__4__	points
Ich fahre mit dem .... nach Leipzig	____	points
Ich fahre mit dem .... nach München	____	points
Ich fahre mit dem .... nach Frankfurt	____	points
Ich fahre mit dem .... nach Köln	____	points
Ich fahre mit dem .... nach Hamburg	____	points
Ich fahre mit dem .... nach Kiel	____	points
Ich fahre mit dem .... nach Berlin	____	points

Wir Spielen Zusammen

Die template for a tour of Germany

This page may be photocopied for use by the purchasing institution only.

Wir Spielen Zusammen

Quiz corners

Question and answer game/test

Objective
- To assess pupils' knowledge of several areas of language or vocabulary as a 'round-up' of a few weeks' work. The teacher can monitor answers orally during the game, or answers can be written down for the whole class to check at the end of the session.

Setting up the game
- In this game the questions can be in English so that the emphasis is on producing the right language in response, rather than trying to understand the question. Alternatively, as pupils become more knowledgable and confident, both questions and answers can be in German.
- Photocopy and cut out the question vocabulary cards (page 50). Fill in the blanks to practise the particular area(s) of vocabulary that you want to assess. Alternatively, pupils could prepare these in advance for others in the class to use. If you play with just one set of cards, the pupils will have to return them so that other pairs/groups can also answer those questions. Alternatively, if you prepare several sets of cards, pupils could keep the cards and write their answers on them.
- Pupils work in pairs or small groups.

How to play the game
1. Designate the four corners of the classroom as the four 'quiz corners' (or if this is not feasible, four table tops, four trays or boxes). Using four separate areas makes it more interesting than a 'sit-down' test as pupils have to move between the areas and their 'bases'.
2. Name each corner with the first four letters of the German alphabet.
3. Place an equal amount of cards in each of the four corners.
4. Player one chooses a corner at random. Player two has to pick up a card from there and ask player one the question written on the card. Player two then returns the card to the bottom of the pile he/she took it from (if you are playing with just one set of cards).
5. It is now the turn of player two to pick a corner, from which player one has to pick up a question card.
6. If the card chosen has already been answered, the players must still answer the question again before continuing. The fact that some cards may be repeatedly picked up in the attempt to find them all is beneficial as it gives pupils extra practice through repetition.
7. The game can be made competitive by setting a time limit within which the pair/group answering the most questions correctly wins. Alternatively the winning pair/group is the one which completes all the questions first.

Extension/variation
- Each corner could be used to practise a different theme, for example, weather in the 'A' corner, classroom items in the 'B' corner, days of the week in the 'C' corner, etc. Alternatively all the areas could have the same theme.

Corner question vocabulary cards

1. What is _____ in German?	2. What is _____ in German?	3. What is _____ in German?
4. What is _____ in German?	5. What is _____ in German?	6. What is _____ in German?
7. What is _____ in German?	8. What is _____ in German?	9. What is _____ in German?
10. What is _____ in German?	11. What is _____ in German?	12. What is _____ in German?

This page may be photocopied for use by the purchasing institution only.

Wir Spielen Zusammen

Rock, paper, scissors

Question and answer game/test

Objective
- To test vocabulary or spelling using the 'rock, paper, scissors' hand game – more fun than writing down answers to a list of questions! (It can be used to practise any language area.)

```
Schlüsselwörter – Key words
Fels (m)         rock
Papier (n)       paper
Schere (f)       scissors
```

Setting up the game
- You can use the cards from 'quiz corners' (page 50) and the spelling cards (page 52). You will need two types of questions – ones which ask for an **oral response**, e.g. 'What is the German word for "cheese"?' and ones which ask the players to **spell** a word, e.g. 'Spell the word for "cheese" in German'. Alternatively questions can be in German, e.g. 'Was heißt "cheese" auf Deutsch?' or 'Wie schreibt man "cheese" auf Deutsch?'
- Players sit in pairs around a table with the question cards in two piles in the middle. They need paper to record scores and for written responses.

How to play the game
1. On the count of three in German they each put out one hand, with the hand made into one of three shapes – **rock** which is the fist clenched into a ball shape, **paper** which is a flat hand palm downwards, or **scissors** which is the forefinger and middle finger opening and closing (like scissors). If you wish, you could use the German words for 'rock, paper, scissors' (see key words).
2. A player wins the round in the following ways:
   - 'paper' beats 'rock'
   - 'rock' beats 'scissors'
   - 'scissors' beats 'paper'
3. If both players have chosen the same hand shape, then there is no winner for that round and they must play again.
4. Whoever wins a round answers a question.
   - If he won using 'paper', his opponent asks him to **write down** a word.
   - If he won using 'rock', he has to **answer a question orally**.
   - If he won using 'scissors' he can cut his opponent's score back by one point, or he can opt for a question that his opponent chooses.
5. Answering questions correctly will get 2 points, incorrectly 0 points.
6. The winner is the player who has the most points at the end of a time limit, or when all the questions have been used up, whichever is most suitable.

Extension/variation
- Without using written question cards or point scoring, this game works well as a warm-up, a way of players testing each other orally on any subject they wish. It also works well as a time filler at the end of a lesson. Players do the 'rock, paper, scissors' actions and the winner answers questions as before, but they could be anything thought up by their partner, or from a particular theme or vocabulary list.

Spelling cards

1. How do you spell _____ in German?	2. How do you spell _____ in German?	3. How do you spell _____ in German?
4. How do you spell _____ in German?	5. How do you spell _____ in German?	6. How do you spell _____ in German?
7. How do you spell _____ in German?	8. How do you spell _____ in German?	9. How do you spell _____ in German?
10. How do you spell _____ in German?	11. How do you spell _____ in German?	12. How do you spell _____ in German?

This page may be photocopied for use by the purchasing institution only.

www.ingramcontent.com/pod-product-compliance
Lightning Source LLC
Chambersburg PA
CBHW081351160426
43197CB00015B/2724